FOREWORD

"Overhearing a conversation about International Women's Day in the Library in late spring of 2024, gave me the inspiration to create this piece of work to celebrate and commemorate the lives of four remarkable women who lived in Dronfield.

Starting with a blank sheet of paper, I researched records from many different sources including Dronfield Heritage Trust documents and photographs, BMD and Census records, newspaper reports, books, museums and getting in touch with living relatives of some of the women featured. I was able to develop the life stories of the women for you to be able to learn about today, so we can remember them, and the contribution of many women past and present, to the way we live our lives today.

I trust that you will enjoy reading about these remarkable women as much as I enjoyed researching their lives."

Andrew Turner
Dronfield Heritage Trust

Sarah Elizabeth Outram

Sarah Elizabeth Outram was born in Dronfield on 20th October 1868 and along with older brother, Samson Mason born in 1867 and later a sister, Margaret born in 1872, lived with their parents, Samuel and Emma in Mill Lane, Dronfield.

In the 1871 Census, Samuel is recorded as a Miller and Farmer of 19 acres living in Mill Lane, Dronfield

(No:1, Mill Lane as seen from Chesterfield Road)

By 1881 census Samuel had become a Grocer and Sarah is recorded as a 12 years old scholar. (at Dronfield Board School)

At the completion of her formal education, she stayed on at school as a Pupil-Teacher. Sarah was clearly quite a clever girl to be allowed to remain at School Lane.

When she was old enough, she attended the Teacher Training College in Cheltenham. She qualified at the end of 1890 and took up a position of school mistress in Sedbergh, Yorkshire.

The Sedbergh and District Parish Magazine January 1891 issue reported that *"the Managers of Sedbergh National School have appointed Miss Outram, from the Training College at Cheltenham to succeed Miss Hill, who retired in November 1890. Miss Outram has passed through her preparation with great credit and has shown marked ability in her profession."*

Sedburgh National school

On the 5th April 1891, the Census was taken and Sarah is stated as being a Boarder, living with John Kilshaw (a tailor) and his wife, Elizabeth at Settlebeck Cottages, Sedbergh, (occupation: School mistress) close to the school where she taught.

Settlebeck cottages

After approximately 18 months in Sedbergh, Sarah decided to move back to Dronfield.

The Sedbergh and District Parish Magazine October 1892 issue reported that *"All friends of the Sedbergh*

National School will regret to hear that Miss Outram, the mistress of the Junior Department is leaving Sedbergh having been elected to a post in the school in which she formally served as Pupil Teacher. Her kindness and firmness of character has won her the respect of all the children"

Sarah moved back in with her parents at Mill Lane in September 1892 commenced teaching at School Lane on the 3rd October and made an entry in the school log as follows:

> 1892
>
> Oct. 3rd I, Sarah Elizabeth Outram, commenced duties this morning as Head Mistress.
>
> Introduced practice of marking registers at 9 o'clock punctually, the late scholars being admitted after prayers. Out of the 246 scholars on books only 65 received the early mark which is made with red ink. The second and final closing for the morning meeting is 9.40.
>
> Found classes and staff arranged thus:—
>
> | Standard | No. of child | Name of Teacher | Qualific. of same |
> |---|---|---|---|
> | 5, 6 & 7 | 34 | Miss Smell | Ex. P.T. |
> | 4 | 40 | Miss Beaver | Ex. P.T. |
> | 3 | 47 | Miss Vaughan | Certific. assist. |
> | 2 | 53 | Miss Ward | P.T. end of 4yr |
> | 1 | 66 | Florence Lockward | Monitress |
>
> Resolved to devote what time I could spare from superintendance to the teaching of standard 1.

Records from the 1901 Census show that Sarah aged 32 years, a Certificated School Teacher was still living at Mill Lane with her father, Samuel Outram, a retired miller aged 64 years and mother, Emma aged 70 years. The next four years were a difficult time for Sarah as firstly her father died in 1902 followed by her mother in 1905.

Samuel and Emma are buried together in Dronfield parish churchyard.

Miss Outram, far right, and some of her pupils in about 1910

After her parents died, Sarah moved from of the family home in Mill Lane to 13, Chesterfield Road, where in the 1911 Census she is recorded as 42 years old, single and an Elementary Teacher.

Trouble ahead for Miss Outram

In 1914, a very concerned father sent a letter to the school teaching his young child. His concern was that 'sexual instruction' had been given to his 11-year-old daughter by Miss Outram, Headmistress of the Girls Department at Dronfield School, the teacher was taking a radical approach to sex education and teaching the girls herself.

The lesson complained about was meant to be one of scripture. But as the class progressed, Miss Outram was asked a series of inquisitive questions by her girls. At first, she told them to ask their mothers: 'she is the proper person to tell you'.

In response the Headmistress read them two short stories, far from controversial from a 21st century perspective. The first used religious ideas and seeds to discuss the ideas of childbirth; The other focused more on chastity and self-control, suggesting relationships and sex were not things to be rushed into.

Neither story explicitly mentioned sex or sexual acts, however in the context of the Edwardian period this was very controversial. At the turn of the century, various social movements supported sexual purity, hygiene and feminism; all of which pushed for more sex education for various different reasons. In this era, the conversation around sexual education often also linked into conversations around eugenics and limiting population size.

There was no formal or standardised sex education in schools at this time. Just talking about sex and relationships, even in these vague terms, was feared to have the potential to corrupt the young girls' minds.

The girls went home and mentioned it to their families and the message spread. The sexual instruction in question was claimed to be various things, indeed some parents even refused to speak of it when asked, so sensational it was thought to be.

There appears to have been very little knowledge of what was actually said. One father noted:
'Mrs Penn, I shall not let our Betty come while Miss Outram is in the school. She has not told me what she [Miss Outram] has said, but I shall not let her come.' Multiple testimonies from the 11-, 12- and 13-year-olds were recorded and describe some of what they were told. One 12-year-old girl mentioned various things that Miss Outram had recounted previously, including telling the girls about breast-feeding and that 'babies come out of mothers' wombs and they are there nine months before they mature'.

Miss Outram was not helped by previous criticisms that had been made against her. In February 1911 there had been complaints about her teaching suffragette doctrine. At the time she reassured managers she would not teach controversial subjects in the future.

Parents were so distraught about the sex education received by their girls that only 11 of Miss Outram's 36 pupils attended school.
Some parents were advocating a school strike, but were told that they would face prosecution for keeping their child out of school, if they did so.

This was followed by a mass meeting of concerned parents and local residents, and a resolution was passed for Miss Outram to resign. A petition was signed by 1,220 inhabitants of Dronfield.

She did not resign!

Miss Outram also received over 300 letters of support, one from the progressive local campaigner and free love advocate, Edward Carpenter.

Miss Outram made this statement in January 1914 at a School Managers' meeting:

'I acknowledge it is a mistake. I will be more careful in future. It is a lovely little story all the same and there is no harm in it. We all make mistakes. I was not willfully doing anything wrong, if I have done anything wrong. I do not acknowledge that I have done anything wrong.'

Two things were in Miss Outram's favour, the tensions between the local and county Education boards (the Derby County Education Board was not keen to intervene) and the First World War. On the outbreak of war, the Board of Education closed the file, without a resolution to the problem, as more pressing matters had taken precedence.

Parents would have been shocked to find out about Miss Outram's wider political beliefs. In 1918 she was not only present at, but chaired, a meeting of 300 teachers and women students at the Cutlers' Hall, Sheffield to talk about equal pay for equal work in the teaching profession. The meeting was organised by the Women's Party (which had developed out of the Suffragette organisation, the Women's Social and Political Union, or WSPU) with the key speaker being the Suffragette leader Emmeline Pankhurst.

Many teachers were part of the women's suffrage movement and Miss Outram personally contributed to the funds of the WSPU, the militant faction of the women's suffrage movement.

The reaction to Miss Outram's stories is an example of how controversial sex education was for young girls at this time. It shows a fear of female empowerment, and illustrates the slowly changing world for women and girls.

Miss Outram, 1914

Miss Outram 1914

Miss Outram remained in her post as Headmistress for another six years until 1922 when she was forced to resign. The period 1920-22 was very difficult for the Girls' school, one member of staff was frequently absent with a nervous breakdown and another with heart attacks. Visits from His Majesty's Inspector of Schools followed and eventually on 27th July 1922, Miss Outram was given her notice to expire on 31st October, she said "when I shall have completed 30 years of faithful service".

However, this was not the end for Sarah as another phase of her life was about to start with the results of local elections. The Derbyshire Times, Saturday 31st March 1923 printed a letter from Sarah as follows:

To the electors of the Dronfield Urban District Council

Ladies and Gentlemen,
May I thank the 260 voters of the town of Dronfield who have elected me as their first ever woman representative on the Urban District Council, and who, by so doing, have shown their disagreement with my having been given six months notice of dismissal after 30 years of faithful service, during which I always had as my chief consideration the present and future welfare of my pupils?
I repeat my promise to serve the interests of the Dronfield ratepayers with that earnest endeavour which has characterised my public work in the past: and if, as Councillor, I can be of personal use, I shall be pleased so long as it is consistent with my sense of right.
Yours faithfully,
S.E. OUTRAM
27th March 1923

Miss Outram's continued to serve the town of Dronfield for a further 17 years until 3rd April 1939, when she finally retired after 47 years of public service as both a teacher and a councillor. She had moved to "Aston View" Lea Road in 1928 and the 1939 Register confirms her address and gave her occupation solely as "retired teacher" not "retired Councillor" as if to re-inforce being harshly treated by the Education authorities.

Miss Sarah Elizabeth Outram, never married and lived on her own at "Aston View" for another 11 years until her death on 17th March 1950 aged 81 years.

The post mortem held on 20th March 1950 by the Coroner for the Hundred of Scarsdale, Derbyshire recorded a verdict of "death by misadventure" and stated that the cause of death was from "shock due to a fractured skull sustained when she fell down the cellar steps at home"

It is not known where Sarah was finally laid to rest

Sources :

BMD Records

Census Records

Dronfield Heritage Trust Archives

Dronfield Miscellany Issue 13 Spring/ Summer 2007

The Derbyshire Courier Saturday 7th February 1914

Michelle Hartley   Sedbergh and District History Society

Dronfield Eye Magazine Issue 167 September 2019

The Derbyshire Times Saturday 31st March 1923

Narrative by William j. Don Outram held at National Archives

Charlotte Mary Ward

Charlotte Mary Ward was born on the 12th November 1889 in Hoyland, Barnsley. She was the 4th child of John Ward and his wife, Mary Noble.

Their other children were:

Charlotte born 1883 died 1884.

Thomas Sykes born 1886 died 1909.

Charles Harold born 1888 died 1968.

Charlotte Mary born 1889 died 1971.

Fanny Elizabeth Mildred born 1894 died 1936.

Charlotte Mary's birth record, 1889

In the 1891 Census, the Ward's were living on King Street, Nether Hoyland where John was a Grocer and Draper, despite being born in Unstone to a well-established farming family, owners of a substantial amount of land around Dronfield, Unstone, Cowley and Barlow. John's father, Thomas and brother, Sykes managed the farm land for many years until Thomas died in 1868, upon which Sykes continued to look after the farms. John had a share of the farming land, but continued in his occupation of Grocers assistant in Hoyland. He had lived with John and Martha Knowles above their Grocers' shop for many years in Hoyland village and later in 1881 moved to Stubbin Lane, Nether Hoyland with John and Martha.

He was 43 years old at this time, however a year later in 1882, he met and married Mary Noble, 16 years his junior, daughter of Thomas and Mary Noble, also Grocer's in the town. At King Street, Hoyland they had Thomas Sykes, Charles Harold and Charlotte Mary aged 4 years, 3 years and 1 year respectively. Fanny Elizabeth was also born there in 1894.

On 8th May 1891, John's brother, Sykes died unmarried and left almost everything he owned to John (Charlotte's father) including all the farm land in the area around Dronfield, thus elevating John to Trustee of the family estates.

King Street, Hoyland 1891

The Ward's moved to Unstone after Fanny had been born in 1894.

When the 1901 Census was recorded, the Ward family were living on Unstone Lane, Unstone, the property was called "Midland House". John aged 61 years is stated as living by "Own Means" along with wife, Mary aged 44 years, Thomas Sykes aged 14 years, Charles Harold aged 13 years, Charlotte Mary aged 11 years and Fanny aged 7 years.

Photograph taken between 1904 and 1909 at the property of Henry Hitch who was living at the time at 22, Clarkegrove Road, Sheffield

Back row: Charlotte Mary Ward, Thomas Sykes Ward, Charles Harold Ward, Fanny Elizabeth Mildred Ward, William Henry Hitch.

Front row: unknown, Henry Hitch (Charlotte's first cousin, once removed), Richard White Hitch, Mary Elizabeth Hitch (Charlotte's first cousin and Henry's second wife), Charlotte Elizabeth Hitch.

1909 was a sad year for all as Thomas Sykes Ward aged 23 years committed "suicide by shooting himself with a revolver whilst of unsound mind" at Chesterfield Road, Greenhill Moor, Norton on 16th or 17th August 1909.

An inquest was held on 19th August by Albert Green, coroner for the Hundred of Scarsdale who determined the cause of death. Thomas is buried in Dronfield Cemetery, grave plot AJ119.

By 1911, the rest of the family, remained together and are recorded as still living at Midland House, Unstone but less than a year later on 2nd December 1912, John died aged 73 years. His estate, which he bequeathed to his son, Charles Harold was valued at £25000, which would have the equivalent buying power of £3.5 million today.

In 1916, Charles Harold enlisted in the Army Veterinary Corps as a Horse keeper and gave his occupation as Trustee.

In the 1921 census, Mary Ward and her son Charles, were recorded as still living at Midland House, 361 Chesterfield Road, however Charlotte's whereabouts are not known.

Charlotte's sister Fanny Elizabeth had married Francis Frederick Howell, an electrical engineer in October 1919 and they lived at Southwood Farm, Hill Top. In 1931 they had a daughter, also called Charlotte Mary. Sadly in 1936, Fanny died aged 41 years in Belfast possibly in childbirth. There is mention of baby Pearl on Fanny's gravestone (neither her birth or death are registered so we can assume that Pearl was stillborn).

Charlotte Mary aged 47 years then became Guardian for her sister's daughter (also Charlotte) aged 6 years and tagged the Ward surname on to her name, thus becoming Charlotte Mary Howell Ward. She had her niece educated and she went on to become a theological student.

Following the death of their mother, Mary in 1938, Charlotte Mary, her brother, Charles Harold and niece, Charlotte moved from Midland House to Cliffe House, Green Lane, the former home of Dr Rooth, a well-known local doctor.

Cliffe House, early 20th century

In the 1939 Register at Cliffe House, Green Lane are Charlotte M Ward whose occupation is given as "Estate Management and Household Duties" and Charlotte M H Ward "at school".

On 7th January 1957, Charlotte Mary Howell Ward died suddenly at Cliffe House aged just 25 years from Acute pulmonary oedema and Acute Bronchiolitis (breathing difficulties commonly caused by a viral infection). Thereafter, Charlotte Ward kept her niece's bedroom locked up leaving it exactly as it was when her niece died. Years later when the house was sold following Charlotte's death, contractors had to break open the bedroom door and found dresses still hanging from wardrobe doors and everything covered in dust and spider's webs. Dresses and bed linen crumbled at the slightest touch.

In April 1960, Charlotte was locked in a battle with both the G.P.O. and Yorkshire Electricity over telegraph poles and electricity supply running over and under her land. At various time she was described as "arrogant" and "dictatorial" by State industry and local authority. She would not have a telephone in her rambling mansion as she considered it "an instrument of the devil which allowed perfect strangers to intrude on one's privacy". She was a very determined lady and even conducted her own case at a public enquiry over trees cut down on her land by GPO and YEB without her permission and won!

Charlotte was a stickler for protocol, one Spring evening in 1960 when her battle with YEB was at it's height, a large group of Press, TV and Radio personnel besieged Cliffe House, so she sent her man to the door to request visiting cards- only one reporter had a card and this was taken into the house on a traditional silver tray, The reporter from The Derbyshire Times was the only Press man to get an interview. He was treated with the utmost courtesy, given some fine old Madeira wine in an exquisite piece of Venetian glass, which Miss Ward claimed had been brought back from Italy by an ancestor and every question put to her by the reporter was meticulously answered.

To many in Dronfield, Charlotte and her brother appeared to be a strange couple and were continually tormented by stone throwing youths at the rear of their property which backed on to Cliffe Park.

On the 11th February 1968, Charles Harold died aged 80 years at Cliffe House and left almost £37,000 to Charlotte. On his grave it says "He befriended all helpless and hunted creatures, and they trusted him".

Charlotte Mary Ward died on 18th March 1971 aged 82 years at Cliffe House. She was laid to rest with other members in their family grave in Dronfield Cemetery.

Grave plots AJ104 & 105, Dronfield Cemetery

In the High Court of Justice

The District Probate Registry at SHEFFIELD

BE IT KNOWN that CHARLOTTE MARY WARD of The Cliffe 2 Green Lane Dronfield Derbyshire

died on the 18th day of March 1971

domiciled in England and Wales

AND BE IT FURTHER KNOWN that at the date hereunder written the last Will and Testament

(a copy whereof is hereunto annexed) of the said deceased was proved and registered in the District Probate Registry of the High Court of Justice at SHEFFIELD and Administration of all the estate which by law devolves to and vests in the personal representative of the said deceased was granted by the aforesaid Court to WILLIAMS & GLYN'S TRUST COMPANY LIMITED of 5 Church Street Sheffield by virtue of the Williams & Glyn's Bank Act 1970 and GRAHAM LILLYMAN of 72 Ridgeway Drive Sheffield the executors named in the said Will

and it is hereby certified that an Inland Revenue affidavit has been delivered wherein it is shown that the gross value of the said estate in Great Britain
 exclusive of what the said deceased may have been possessed of or entitled to as a trustee and not beneficially amounts to £ 16,673.75
and that the net value of the estate amounts to £ 16,446.47
and it is further certified that it appears by a receipt signed by an Inland Revenue officer on the said affidavit that £ 60,917.19 on account of estate duty and interest on such duty has been paid.

Dated the 8th day of December 1971

Dh Jackson
District Registrar

Extracted by Stanton and Walker, Solicitors, Chesterfield.

The probate of Charlotte Mary Ward

This is the last Will and Testament

of me

CHARLOTTE MARY WARD of The Cliffe 2 Green Lane Dronfield in the County of Derby Spinster

1. I APPOINT Williams Deacons Bank Limited and Graham Lilleyman of 72 Ridgeway Drive in the City of Sheffield (hereinafter called "my Trustees") to be the Executors and Trustees of this my Will AND I DECLARE that the said Williams Deacons Bank Limited may act as such Executor and Trustee upon the terms and conditions specified in the Bank's published Trustee Prospectus in force at the date hereof with the right to remuneration in accordance with the said Bank's published Scale of Fees in force at the date of my death and with power to charge remuneration in accordance with any later published Scale of Fees of the said Bank for the time being in force

2. I DESIRE that Stanton & Walker of 12 Soresby Street Chesterfield be employed as Solicitors in connection with my estate without prejudice to my Trustees' right to employ any other Solicitor if it should be considered expedient

3. I GIVE AND BEQUEATH the following legacies (all free of duty) namely:-
To Mrs. Margaret Goodall of 6 Elm Tree Crescent Dronfield in recognition of her loyal and devoted service to me the sum of Two thousand pounds
To Leonard Goodall (the Son of Mrs. Margaret Goodall) the sum of One hundred pounds
To Mrs. Joan Christina Kenny of 18 Ethelbert Road Canterbury the sum of Two thousand pounds
To Mrs. Joan Ditchfield of Unstone Farm Unstone near Sheffield the sum of One hundred pounds
To Mrs. Freda Roberts of 60 Norfolk Street Boston in the County of Lincoln the sum of Three hundred pounds
To Miss Mary A. Goodwin of Hastin Moor near Chesterfield the sum of Three hundred pounds
To Mrs. May Meadows of The Sycamores Cowley Lane Cowley near Dronfield the sum of One hundred pounds
To Vera Kay formerly of The Fish Shop Sheffield Road Dronfield the sum of One hundred pounds
To Shirley Wellard of 31 Harland Avenue Sidcup Kent the sum of One hundred pounds
To Jean Hellivell, the local (Dronfield) Collector for the Royal Society for the Prevention of Cruelty to Animals the sum of One hundred pounds for her own use and benefit absolutely

4. I GIVE AND BEQUEATH to the Dronfield & District Joint Burial Committee (free of duty) the sum of One hundred pounds UPON TRUST that they shall invest the same and shall apply the income thereof in keeping the Cemetery at Dronfield in good order and repair AND I REQUEST such Committee to keep in good order and repair the grave and gravestones of my late Father of my late Mother of my late Niece Charlotte Mary Ward of my late Brother Thomas Sykes Ward of my late Sister Fanny Elizabeth Mildred Ward and of my late Brother Charles Harold Ward and to keep the lettering thereon legible and to cause the lettering to be re-cut from time to time when necessary for that purpose AND I DECLARE that if at any time during the period of Eighty years next ensuing after my death the said grave or gravestones or any of them shall not be kept in good order and repair or the lettering on them shall not be legible or re-cut as aforesaid then the said sum of One hundred pounds or the investment representing the same shall be paid and transferred to The Royal Society for the Prevention of Cruelty to Animals to whom I BEQUEATH the same accordingly

5. I GIVE AND DEVISE to the said Graham Lilleyman (free of duty) my freehold dwellinghouse land and premises known as The Cliffe 2 Green Lane Dronfield and the garden orchard grounds and buildings appurtenant thereto in fee simple for his own use and benefit but SUBJECT to and charged with the payment of an Annuity of Two hundred and fifty pounds to be paid to The Royal Society for the Prevention of Cruelty to Animals on my birthday the Twelfth day of November in every year AND I HEREBY CHARGE my said property known as The Cliffe 2 Green Lane Dronfield with the payment of the said Annuity in exoneration of the rest of my estate AND I DIRECT

that the said Annuity shall be paid clear of all deductions

6. I GIVE AND BEQUEATH such of my personal chattels as defined by Section 55 (1) (x) of the Administration of Estates Act 1925 as are specified in a list which will be found in a sealed envelope addressed to my Trustees in my Deeds Box to the persons designated in such list AND I GIVE AND BEQUEATH the remainder of my personal chattels so defined as aforesaid to the said Graham Lilleyman for his own use and benefit absolutely

7. I GIVE AND DEVISE (free of duty) to my Tenant Archibald Charles Lee my freehold dwellinghouse land and premises known as Grindlegate Half Acre Lane Unstone and the field known as The Wrangles of which he is now my tenant and my range of old coke ovens and the Burn meadow in which they stand in fee simple

8. PROVIDED that (i) no sale of the real estate devised by this clause of my Will shall take place within a period of five years from the date of my death and (ii) that no Auctioneer Estate Agent or Valuer practising or carrying on business at Chesterfield in the County of Derby be given any instructions or be employed to carry out any work in relation to any of the real estate mentioned in this clause of my Will THEN I GIVE AND DEVISE (free of duty) :-
(a) all my freehold lands in the hamlet of Cowley in the Parish of Holmesfield in the County of Derby including Greenfield Farm, Spa House farmlands, Cowley farmlands, Sloades Farm, Cherry Tree Farm, the bungalow land and premises known as "The Sycamores", the dwellinghouse land and premises known as "Summerley", the land at Cowley Gore known as "the Cow Meadows", Fields Numbers 453, 456, 457 and 477 on the Derbyshire Ordnance Survey Sheet XVII.8 (1898 Edition), the farm buildings known as The Butterpot buildings and the dwellinghouse land and premises known as The Cottage, Cowley (subject to any existing Lease thereof) to The Royal Society for the Prevention of Cruelty to Animals in fee simple
(b) all my freehold lands and premises at Hill Top Dronfield aforesaid including the farm buildings and yard (but not the farmhouse which has been sold) known as Southwood Farm together with the farm lands thereto belonging and the Plantation and the dwellinghouse land and premises known as Southwood House to the National Anti-Vivisection Society Limited (Sheffield Branch) in fee simple
(c) all my freehold lands and premises at Unstone in the said County of Derby including the farmlands let to Mr. Hunt, the house buildings and land let to Mr. Ditchfield and the field known as The Barn Croft to The People's Dispensary for Sick Animals (Heeley, Sheffield Branch) in fee simple
(d) my four fields of freehold land containing approximately Forty acres or thereabouts at Apperknowle in the said County of Derby to The League against Cruel Sports Limited (Huddersfield Branch) in fee simple

9. I GIVE AND BEQUEATH all the residue of my personal estate not previously or specifically disposed of by this my Will to my Trustees UPON TRUST to sell call in and convert the same into money at such time or times and in such manner as they shall think fit with full power in their absolute discretion to postpone the sale calling in and conversion of the whole or any part or parts thereof for so long as they shall think proper without being responsible for loss and with and out of the moneys thereby produced and with and out of my ready money to pay my just debts funeral and testamentary expenses and all estate and other duties and taxes payable on my death (including all Estate Duty and Capital Gains Tax payable in respect of my real estate) and the before mentioned pecuniary legacies and to stand possessed of the residue of such moneys IN TRUST to pay and divide the same unto and equally between the following four charitable organisations (hereinafter called "the said Charities") namely:-
The Royal Society for the Prevention of Cruelty to Animals
The National Anti-Vivisection Society Limited (Sheffield Branch)
The People's Dispensary for Sick Animals (Heeley, Sheffield Branch) and
The League against Cruel Sports Limited (Huddersfield Branch)

10. I GIVE AND DEVISE all the residue of my real estate not previously or specifically disposed of by this my Will to my Trustees UPON TRUST to sell call in and convert the same into money at such time or times and in such manner as they shall think fit with full power in their absolute discretion to postpone the sale calling in and conversion of the whole or any part or parts thereof for so long as they shall think proper without being responsible for loss and my Trustees shall stand possessed of the net proceeds of sale of my said residuary estate IN TRUST for The League against Cruel Sports Limited (Huddersfield Branch) absolutely

AND my Trustees shall stand possessed of such part or parts of my residuary real estate as shall for the time being remain unsold UPON TRUST to pay the net income therefrom after deduction of management expenses the cost of repairs maintenance and insurance and such compensation as may be payable to any outgoing tenant (after deduction of any sums recovered from any ingoing tenant) to The League against Cruel Sports Limited (Huddersfield Branch)

11. I DECLARE that the receipts of the Treasurer or other proper officer for the time being of each of the said Charities shall be a good discharge to my Trustees for any sums of money paid to any of the said Charities in accordance with the terms of this my Will without them seeing to the application thereof

12. I DIRECT that out of the moneys which will become payable under this my Will to The Royal Society for the Prevention of Cruelty to Animals a Plaque shall be purchased and erected on some suitable building belonging to The Royal Society for the Prevention of Cruelty to Animals in memory of Charlotte Mary Ward the Younger who loved all animals and who died on 7th January 1957

13. I DECLARE that it is my wish that I shall be buried in the same grave as my Sister Fanny Elizabeth Mildred Ward and my Niece the said Charlotte Mary Ward the Younger in Dronfield Cemetery AND I FURTHER DECLARE that it is my wish that any cats which are being kept by me at the date of my death should be destroyed by The Royal Society for the Prevention of Cruelty to Animals before any other terms of this my Will are carried into effect and if possible before my funeral

14. IN the interpretation of this my Will I DECLARE that all gifts bequests and devises to the Royal Society for the Prevention of Cruelty to Animals shall be construed as if they were for the specific benefit of the Dronfield Branch of such Society, but if there be no such Branch in being at the time of my death then they shall be construed as if they were for the specific benefit of the Chesterfield Branch of such Society

15. I REVOKE all former Wills and testamentary dispositions by me at any time heretofore made

IN WITNESS whereof I the said Charlotte Mary Ward the Testatrix have hereunto set my hand this Fourteenth day of June One thousand nine hundred and sixty eight

Charlotte M. Ward.

SIGNED AND ACKNOWLEDGED by the said Charlotte Mary Ward the Testatrix as and for her last Will and Testament in the presence of us who at her request in her presence and in the presence of each other have hereunto set and subscribed our names as witnesses.

The last will and testament of Charlotte Mary Ward

Charlotte's life long love for all animals was reinforced at the end of her life when the biggest beneficiary of her will was Chesterfield RSPCA, a short statement on their website states:

"A big turning point in our history was an important legacy left by Derbyshire animal lover Charlotte Mary Ward who passed away in the 1970s. She dearly loved all animals and her legacy gave the animal centre £300,000, which at the time expanded the animal centre to care for more than 100 animals. Charlotte's legacy continues to help a lot of animals to this present day".

<u>Resources</u>

Dronfield Heritage Trust Archives

BMD Records

Census Records

The Derbyshire Times

Timeline (Special thanks to Kate Ollerenshaw)

Olive Annie Adlington

Fred Adlington was born on the 18th April 1898 and Beatrice Ethel Bradwell was born on the 13th January 1902, both of them in Dronfield.

The happy couple married in the early summer of 1921 aged 24 years and 19 years respectively, at the Methodist Free Church, High Street, Dronfield. Their married life began living at No 3 Coronation Cottages, Victoria Street, Dronfield close to where Beatrice's parents, Jacob and Ada ran The Victoria Inn.

Olive Annie was born on the 13th March 1922, at No 3 Coronation Cottages and Beatrice registered her daughter's birth in Chesterfield on the 19th April 1922.

Olive's birth record

After marriage, Fred began a business making ice cream and sold it from his converted bicycle, then opened a Fish and Chip Shop in the High Street, before buying a grocery store on Scarsdale Road at the corner of Wilson Street.

1 Wilson Street, Dronfield

Olive, also known as "Bunty" attended Dronfield Council School on School Lane and in September 1932, whilst in Standard 4, the following photo was taken. This photo is from the Dronfield Heritage Trust Archives and although we know most of the names of the girls, they are not identified individually.

Olive's nephew has been able to identify her in the front row, 5th from the left.

Olive was elected Dronfield "Carnival Queen" on 22nd August 1938 at the annual Carnival Queen Dance held at Dronfield Town Hall.

The presentation and crowning of the "Carnival Queen" and her attendants by Mrs Henrietta Jervis Cecil took place at Dronfield Grammar School cricket field on 10th September 1938. Olive was 16 ½ years old

Photograph of Olive in her "Carnival Queen" regalia 1938

In the 1939 Register, Olive is recorded as "Assistant, Grocery and Beer-off" living with her parents and two brothers, John Frederick born 1926 and Donald born 1936 at 1, Wilson Street helping out in the family run shop, which she had probably done for a couple of years after leaving school.

Olive joined the Women's Royal Naval Service (W.R.N.S. Reg No 20423) after her birthday in March 1941 as the minimum age to join the Wrens was 19 years at this time, she trained to be a Telegraphist and Morse code operator whilst on posting in Oban, Scotland.

She would have also learnt about coding and decoding, basic sonar, ASDICS and repairing radio receivers. The training would have been a minimum of 6 months. In June 1943, she was posted to Liverpool, a city heavily bombed by the Luftwaffe and quite a contrast to Scotland. Her initial duties on rota in Liverpool, included working 8-hour night shifts fire-watching from one of the domes above the Liver Building.

After several months, Olive was promoted to Petty Officer and sent to work underground at Derby House, Liverpool, at the Western Approaches Tactical Unit, also known as the "Citadel", a rabbit warren of corridors and rooms of Combined Operations, Navy and Air Force, where the Battle of the Atlantic was planned and organised by Commander-in-Chief Sir Max

Horton. Outside it was fenced, sand-bagged and guarded by sentries. A very secretive place.

In the book, Merseyside at War 1939-45 by Mike Royden, Olive re-counted that she *"was one of many little cogs in a big machine, all around the main plotting room, which had a complete wall of glass, so that the boss could see everything that was going on. The Wireless Office where I worked, had five machines on different frequencies, plus one tape machine which was similar to a typewriter, except it produced ribbons of punched paper and was used to send automatic Morse on long routine messages. The room also had a landline- a type of Morse key connected to Admiralty Plymouth, it was difficult to read, but I soon got the hang of it. Ship to shore was only done in emergencies, as wireless silence was necessary to protect he fleet.*

Most messages sent were general ones only to be acted on if the coded message in the preamble applied to that particular ship or port.

At times reading Morse in all that noise, and with all the atmospheric crackles, was almost to much to bear and a period of clear signals was a huge relief. Long night duties were particularly tiring, especially if there was too much traffic to be able to take a break. A week of nights followed by three weeks of days, the days were OK but the nights nearly killed us! You would be working 8 hours solidly and they say that you shouldn't do Morse for longer than 5 hours as you start making mistakes. A short break if we were lucky! It was during my time in Liverpool that I received my arm stripe for three years service".

A very important part of Olive's duties was to communicate by Morse with Allied ships, Merchant and Naval, as they came in and left for the Mersey estuary, guiding them on direction and speed so as to avoid German submarines and surface vessels.

Olive continued *"After four years though, the war was over and we were discharged, it was quite an anti-climax and we were just left to get on with life as best we could.*

There was no counseling in those days and it was so difficult to settle back in to civilian life. I received £45 and 8 shillings as a War Gratuity".

On 1st January 1946, Olive was awarded the British Empire Medal in the Military New Years Honours List for her "meritorious" wartime service. She received the Medal along with a letter from the King dated 13th May 1947.

"Meritorious service" in wartime is described as:

a single, particular important achievement, or a career notable for accomplishments in technical or professional fields or unusually high quality and initiative in leadership.

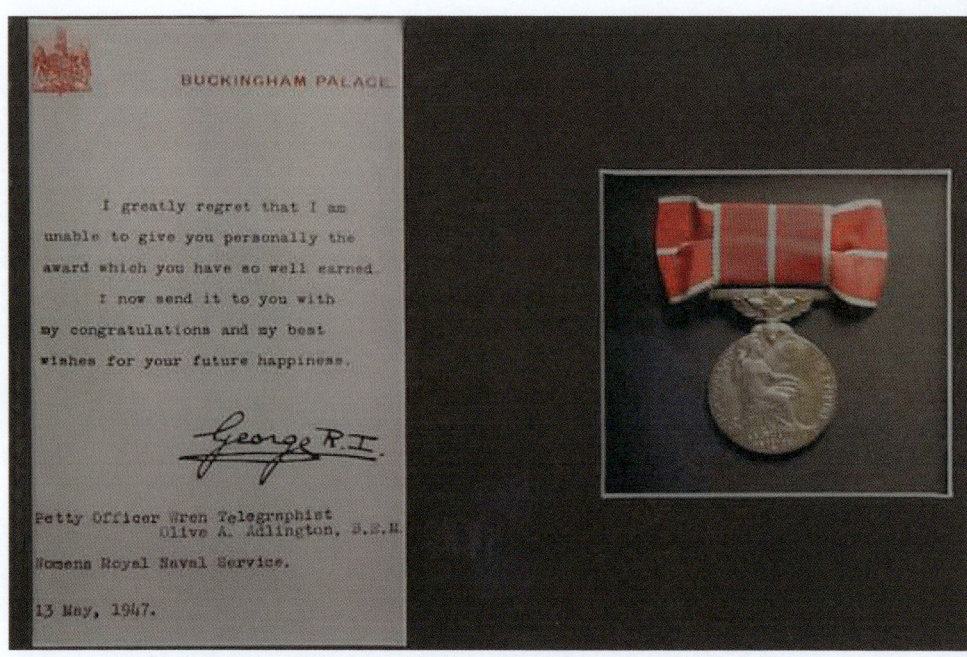

Letter of commendation from Buckingham Palace, 13 May 1947

SUPPLEMENT TO THE LONDON GAZETTE, 1 JANUARY, 1946

Robert KIRKWOOD, Esq. Assistant Superintendent, Posts and Telegraphs Department, British North Borneo. For services during internment.
William Allan LAMBERT, Esq. For services in connection with leprosy in Tanganyika.
Stuart LOWRIE, Esq. For services during internment in Malaya.
Arthur McCOLM, Esq. For services during internment in Malaya.
Sybil Kathleen, Mrs. MACKENZIE. For services at Tan Tock Seng Hospital, Singapore.
John Alexander MALIN, Esq. Assistant Secretary, City Council, Gibraltar.
Noel James Linnington MARGETSON, Esq., M.D., F.R.C.S.Ed. Medical Officer, District No. 1 and Medical Officer of Health, Montserrat, Leeward Islands.
M'NGAINE WA M'ITERIA, Chief of the Meru, Kenya.
Miss Glendowra Rosalie MUTTON. Colonial Nursing Service, Senior Nursing Sister, Medical Department, Gold Coast.
Dorothy, Mrs. NEWELL. For public service in the Windward Islands.
Frank Victor NUNES, Esq. For Civil Defence services in Jamaica.
Henry Rupert Carlton PARNALL, Esq. For services during internment in the Far East.
Sidney Norman PETERS, Esq. Chief Clerk, Secretariat, St. Helena.
Nicos ROUSSOS, Esq. Municipal Engineer, Limassol, Cyprus.
Albert SAUVAGE, Esq. For public services in Seychelles.
Aloysius SEQUEIRA, Esq. Office Superintendent, Aden.
Douglas Alkins SKAN, Esq., M.R.C.S., L.R.C.P. Colonial Medical Service, Pathologist, Nyasaland.
Hugh SMITH, Esq., M.B., Ch.B. For services during internment in Malaya.
Helena May, Mrs. SPRAGUE. For welfare services in Kenya.
KOW TAI, Chief Theatre Dresser, Tan Tock Seng Hospital, Singapore. For services during internment.
Joanna Mooney, Mrs. TALLENTIRE. For welfare services in Nigeria.
Harry Alan TAYLOR, Esq., F.R.I.C. Colonial Chemical Service, Assistant Superintendent and Government Chemist, Imports and Exports Department, Hong Kong. For services during internment.
Olunwale James Vonbrunn TUBOKU-METZGER, Esq. Police Magistrate, Sierra Leone.
Frederick Cornelius VAN ZEVLEN, Esq. Director, Public Works Department, Bahamas.
AISEA VASUTOGA, Roko of Nadroga Province, Fiji.
Margaret Jean Howieson, Mrs. WHITE. For services during internment in Malaya.
Miss Elsie Clara WILLIS. For services during internment in Malaya.
William de Weever WISHART, Esq., M.B., C.M. Municipal Health Officer, British Guiana.
James Topp Nelson YANKAH, Esq. For services to education, Gold Coast.
Edith Margaret, Mrs. YATES. For social welfare services in Nigeria.

To be Honorary Members of the Civil Division of the said Most Excellent Order:—
Ismail ABOKER, Esq., Assistant in the Veterinary Department, British Somaliland.

QAID AHMED SUDQI AL JUNDI, Arab Legion.
Xavier Elpidio ALMEIDA, Esq., Chief Clerk, Public Works Department, Uganda.
Jude BELIAVSKY, Esq., Accountant, Palestine.
Isiah Claudius DUBING, Esq., Assistant Accountant, Treasury, Nigeria.
ABDEL AZIZ SHAKER EL DAOUDI, Judge of District Court, Palestine.
KORAM BIN ENDUAT, British North Borneo Constabulary.
Mrs. Shifa FAIZ. For meritorious services in Cyprus.
MUNIR KHALIL MISHALANY, Esq., M.D., Assistant Senior Medical Officer, Palestine.
OMWAMI DAUDI BENEDICTO MUSOKE, County Chief, South Bugishu, Uganda.
OLAOSEBIKAN ADEBAYO OMOLOLU, Tax Officer, Inland Revenue Department, Nigeria.
Emmanuel Chukwuemeka PHILLIPS, Esq., Supervising Teacher, Nigeria.
Samuel Adekunle PRIDDY, Esq., Office Assistant, Agricultural Department, Nigeria.
Hamed SALEH. Liwali of Dar-es-Salaam, Tanganyika Territory.
Joseph SAPHIR, Esq. Mayor of Petah Tiqva, Palestine.

CENTRAL CHANCERY OF THE ORDERS OF KNIGHTHOOD.
St. James's Palace, S.W.1.
1st January, 1946.

The KING has been graciously pleased to make the following appointment to the Order of the Companions of Honour:—

To be a Member:—
Professor Archibald Vivian HILL, O.B.E., Sc.D., D.Sc., LL.D., F.R.S., a Secretary of the Royal Society. For scientific services.

CENTRAL CHANCERY OF THE ORDERS OF KNIGHTHOOD
St. James's Palace, S.W.1.
1st January, 1946.

The KING has been graciously pleased to approve the award of the British Empire Medal (Military Division) to the undermentioned:—

Regulating Petty Officer Joseph Luis ABRAHAM, T.R.N.V.R.11087.
Chief Petty Officer Albert Henry ABRAHAMS, D/J.4185.
Petty Officer Wren Telegraphist Olive Annie ADLINGTON, 20243. W.R.N.S.
Petty Officer Sheikh AHMED, 6936, R.I.N.
Chief Stoker William AITKEN, P/K.60406.
Marine Anthony Francis ALCOR, CH/X.113783.
Petty Officer Albert William ALDERMAN, P/J.763.
Chief Petty Officer Stanley Ernest Hill ALEXANDER, D/J.94522.
Temporary Chief Petty Officer Samuel John ALLEN, D/JX.390251.
Stoker First Class Diver B. ANDREWS, 7764, R.I.N.
Petty Officer Wren Jessica Maud ANDREWS, 30769, W.R.N.S.
Chief Yeoman of Signals Charles William ASHLEY, C/J.41868.
Electrical Artificer 3rd Class Arthur Albert BAILEY, C/MX.65939.
Chief Petty Officer Cook Thomas Raymond Lillicrop BAKER, D/M.37972.

Petty Officer Wren Telegraphist Olive Annie Adlington
WRNS 20243

After the War, Olive trained to be an Infant school teacher and worked in several different schools in the Midlands and the South of England before returning home to teach at Killamarsh.

Following further training she became a Home Economics teacher at the former Edwin Swale school in Chesterfield. Olive moved to Christchurch near Bournemouth to be near to her younger brother and her nieces, when she retired.

Olive would have been bound by The Official Secrets Act and never divulged her true role at Western Approaches Tactical Unit in Liverpool, even to her family, because of its importance to the National Security of this country.

Olive passed away in Bournemouth Hospital on 25th February 2017 aged 94 years

The Plotting Room, Western Approaches Tactical Unit, Liverpool

The Telegraph Office

Sources:

BMD Records   Census records

WRNS Website

Imperial War Museum

Dronfield Heritage Trust Archive

Merseyside at War 1939-45 by Mike Royden

Dronfield Eye Magazine December 2019 Issue 170

The London Gazette Issue 37407 page 64

Western Approaches Tactical Unit Museum Liverpool

The Adlington family

Edith Muriel Gregory

The War Memorial outside the Library on High Street, Dronfield has a number of plaques on its supports remembering more than 70 names of those lost during World War 1 and World War 2. There is only one woman remembered on the Memorial, that of Edith Muriel Gregory who was fatally injured in 1943

Her parents were Harry Frank Gregory and Elizabeth Eyre Jagger, they were married at St. Pauls, Sculcoates on 19th December 1903 aged 20 years and 19 years respectively and lived in Sculcoates, Yorks. His occupation was that of Cooper- a barrel maker.

The 1911 Census shows the Gregory's and their four children were living at 11, Branston Street, Sculcoates.

Harry enlisted on the 5th August 1914 and joined the East Yorkshire Regiment (Reg No 235509) leaving behind a wife and his four children, all under the age of 10. He soon rose through the ranks making Sergeant before being awarded the Military Medal for bravery at the Battle of Piave River, Italy in June 1918. In September 1918, the family moved to 15 Wollaton Avenue, Dansom Lane, Hull. He was demobbed from the Armed Forces in March 1919 and returned to his work as a Cooper with John Hamilton and Co.(Oil Refiners). Sculcoates Bridge, Hull.

Photograph of Harry Frank Gregory and wife Elizabeth, 1914-1917

Edith Muriel, their 6th child and 3rd girl was born at home, 15 Wollaton Avenue, Dansom Lane on 20th January 1921 and registered in Kingston-upon-Hull on 7th March 1921 by her mother, Elizabeth.

Edith Muriels birth record

The 1921 Census shows the Gregory's still living at the same address in Dansom Lane.

Harry Frank	38 yrs	Oil Cooper
Elizabeth	37 yrs	
Arthur	16 yrs	Oil Cooper- Apprentice
Phyllis	11 yrs	Whole Time Education
Henry Francis	10 yrs	Whole Time Education
Herbert	9 yrs	Whole Time Education
Ethel	2 yrs	
Edith Muriel	5mths	

In the early months of 1925, the Gregory's moved again, this time to Dronfield where Harry took the job of Foreman Cooper at Robert Dale Nicol & Co, Manufacturer of Mineral Oil Lubricants on Callywhite Lane, just 10 minutes along the main road to where they all lived at 101, Sheffield Road (next door to Grocutts Grocery and Beer shop)

Former Grocutts shop (the white building). The Gregory home shown on the left of shop demolished late 1960's

Little is known of the schooling of Edith, but it is likely to have been at the Dronfield Cross Lane Board School on School Lane, which was built in 1875, now Dronfield Junior school, which was only half a mile from their home on Sheffield Road.

In 1937, the family move yet again to a semi detached property at No.24 School Lane, Dronfield and her three younger sisters attended the school nearby.

In the 1939 Register, Edith Muriel aged 18 yrs was still living at home and her occupation is listed as Housemaid, domestic service.

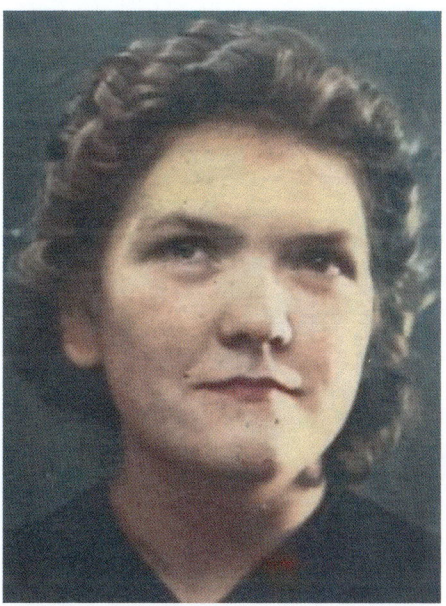

Image of Edith Muriel, late 1930s

On 26th May 1942, she gave up her job as Waitress at The Grand Hotel, Sheffield to answer the call to join The Women's Land Army to work in agriculture to replace the men who had been called up to War duty. She could have applied in writing at a Post Office or by contacting her local WLA County HQ. or she could have been conscripted. Land Army girls could be sent anywhere in the country depending on where they were most needed and were paid 28 shillings per week, (with almost half of her wages going to pay for board and lodgings)

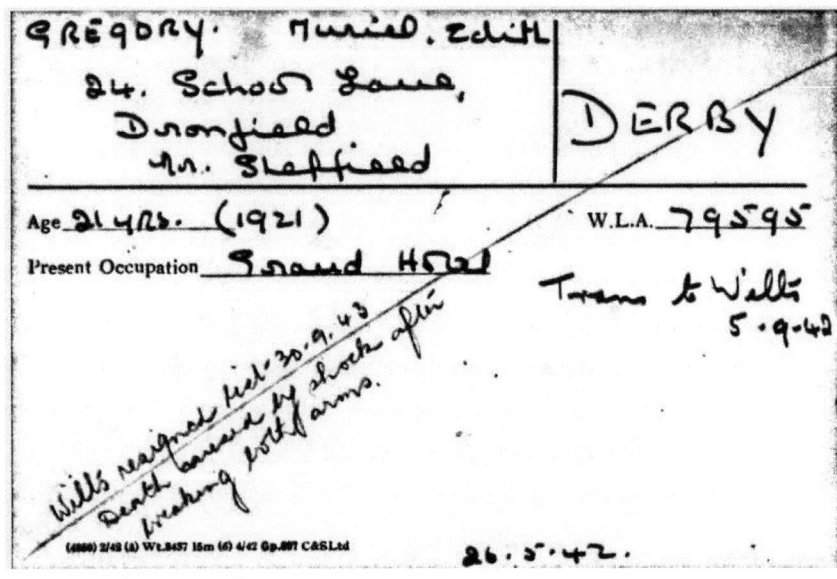

Edith's WWII Women's Land Army Record Card

Sheffield "Grand Hotel", was situated on Leopold Street near to Barkers Pool and demolished in 1974. It would have been easily reached by bus or train from Dronfield.

The contents of a letter from Mrs Anne Hassall, Edith's sister to the Editor of the Dronfield Miscellany was published in Issue 13 and confirms that she worked in Sheffield even though the Land Army card above does not state this fact.

By the end of 1942, 20,000 women and girls had answered the call to join the WLA to assist farmers in all types of agriculture as the need to feed the nation became increasingly more difficult as the months of war dragged on.

The number of women working the land had increased 5-fold by the end of the war.

Edith Muriel (now calling herself Muriel Edith) was transferred to Wiltshire on 5th September 1942 and lodged with Mrs Dorothy Nellie Pearce at 2, Council Houses, Hill Deverill, Wilts, close to her place of employment at Manor Farm.

Her employer, and owner of Manor Farm, was Capt. Edward Robert Courtney Booth, late of the Indian Army and London Stockbroker.

Muriel worked with three men, Bertie Collins, Francis White and Percy Cooper in the fields close to the village for almost a year before a fatal accident ended her short life.

The accident in which Muriel was involved was reported by The Bath Weekly Chronicle and Herald on Saturday 11th September 1943 after the inquest into her death as follows:

Killed in a Wilts cornfield-land girl falls under binder

"A Heroine of the war, 22 years old Edith Muriel Gregory was fatally injured in a Wilts cornfield, which she was helping to reap on 7th August. Previously a waitress in a big hotel, she threw up her job in a great city to join the Land Army, earned two stripes, and became an expert on the farm especially as a tractor driver. "Her death is a loss to the country", the Bath City Coroner (Mr C.S. Elwell) was told at the inquest on Tuesday afternoon when a verdict of Accidental Death was returned. She was employed on the farm of Capt. E.R.C.Booth at Hill Deverill, near Warminster, and was the daughter of a Sheffield nightwatchman. Mrs Pearce, her landlady, with whom she had lodged for nearly a year gave evidence of identification.

The binder had broken down and she was waiting for a spare part to arrive, and with Percy Cooper, farm labourer, stood back at the corner of the wheat to allow the other tractor and binder to go by. Cooper stooped to pick up a couple of sheaves and she must have stepped forward-why he did not know. The first he knew was when he heard the driver cry out. Miss Gregory was entangled in the power drive running from the tractor to the binder. Her clothes wrapped around this and had to be cut off to free her. He could not explain why she should have got in that position. Mr H. Lee (Messrs. Withy, King and Lee, Bath), who represented the employer, ascertained that the pace of the tractor was only three miles an hour.

Another labourer, Francis Patrick White, who was helping to operate the binder, said he never saw Miss Gregory step forward, as he raised the knife, it all happened in practically a split second. The tractor driver, Bertie Collins, said he heard Miss Gregory shout and stopped suddenly. She was "between the bar and over the shaft" – that was, behind him. He could not account for her being in that position, unless she wanted his spanners, and was trying to climb up behind him to ask for them. She might have slipped in doing so. He had no idea that she was going to approach him. It would be risky getting on the tractor. He had never seen it done before.

Dr Patrick Leahy, house surgeon at Royal United Hospital, Bath, said on admission, Miss Gregory was extremely shocked and suffering from a compound fracture of the right upper arm, of both forearms, and of a bone in the face and extensive abrasions covering the back and back of the lower limbs.

Three weeks later, on the evening of 2nd September, she suddenly developed multiple emboli (small blood clots) which affected the lungs and brain and she passed away within an hour. The post-mortem examination showed that these came from an extensive laceration of the right lobe of the liver"

After the Coroner had recorded a verdict of "Accidental Death" Mr Lee, with whom Capt Booth was sitting, expressed Capt Booth's deep sympathy with the relatives of Miss Gregory. Words were quite inadequate to do so, he said. Her untimely death was not only a great loss to her family, but the country had lost one of its war-workers of a very fine type. She had a most excellent character and her passing was a great loss on the farm because she was a fine helper there.

The body was released to Mrs Pearce on instruction from the Coroner and the Death Certificate was issued.

Death record of Edith Muriel

Edith Muriel's funeral took place at Dronfield parish church on 9th September 1943 where the British Legion draped the Union Flag over her coffin. She was buried in Dronfield Cemetery in her older sister, Ethel's grave, she had passed away in 1938 aged 19 years. Their father, Harry Frank was buried there in 1946 (aged 62 years) and their mother was also buried in the same grave in 1970 (aged 86 years)

Burial Plot BA(1)19 - No Headstone survives to mark their passing.

Edith Muriel and her sister Ethel c1925

Happy times, a family together. Mr and Mrs Gregory and their 10 children in the back garden of 24, School Lane, Dronfield c1930

Back row: Arthur, Henry, Phyllis, Elizabeth (mum), Herbert, Harry (dad).

Middle Row: Edith Muriel, Ethel, Annie.

Front Row: Mona, Irene, Betty.

Resources & Credits:

Dronfield Heritage Trust Photo Archive

Land Army Index Cards, Ancestry UK

Women's Land Army website

Census Records

BMD Records

Bath Coroners Inquest Reports 1943

The Bath Weekly Chronicle and Herald Saturday 11th September 1943

Dronfield Eye Directory February 2022

"Neither Silent nor Faceless" by Kate Ollerenshaw

Dronfield Miscellany Issue 13

Grateful thanks to Mrs J Horne and Mr T Horne for the use of their family photographs.

About the Publisher

Thank you for buying this publication. Your purchase supports the Dronfield Heritage Trust in maintaining the Grade II* Listed Dronfield Hall Barn in the heart of our ancient town. The restoration work was completed in 2015 with grant support from the National Lottery Heritage Fund and generous community donations. The Trust maintains the building and grounds with income from the popular Barn Cafe, a lively events programme, arts and heritage exhibitions, publications, and a hospitality business. An army of volunteers works to manage the grounds, welcome visitors, and maintain our archive of local historic documents.

Want to know more? Go to www.dronfieldhallbarn.org and get involved if you can.

Printed in Great Britain
by Amazon